THE THIRD LAW OF SUCCESS™

THE KEY TO LIMITLESS OPPORTUNITY & HIGH ACHIEVEMENT

J. FREDERICK WILSON

J. Frederick Wilson

www.selfgovernment.com

*Pro*Net Publishing
51625 Desert Club Drive
La Quinta, CA 92253

Contents

<u>**Preface**</u>

This manuscript finds its origins in my youth. While growing up I was taught by my parents that the way I looked at my life would in fact shape my life. With that message in mind, they freely gave me books and recordings on the subject of success, and we often discussed the topic. Together they encouraged me that, if I put my mind to it, I could accomplish just about anything. And through their example they showed me what it looked like to get in there and work for it. For those lessons I am ever grateful.

It was during those early experiences that I first began to develop what has become a life long interest in the process of achievement relative to the phenomenon of success. Through my parents' influence it seemed quite natural to me that I should ask questions in life about both subjects. And as I occasionally got the hang of things myself in some respects, a desire followed in me just as naturally that I should share with others what I had learned.

So for more than 40 years—whether in sports, education, sales, or life itself—I have been coaching people how to be their best. Throughout that time my curiosity about the inner workings of achievement has never waned. And along the way the subject of people and their success has grown into one of the great passions of my life. Over time that passion has led me on a journey of discovery that eventually allowed me to break down the fundamental laws of success and identify their supporting principles that are essential to a strong process of achievement. And through those efforts I ultimately discovered something incredible about the experience of success that, during all the preceding years, I had never seen or even heard of before…

Now to be sure, I have failed plenty in my life. Fortunately, though, I have also enjoyed my fair share of success. But whether as a young, aspiring tennis pro who struggled with one of the most important swings in the game—the "mental stroke"—or as a seasoned and top producing sales professional who, having employed the right mindset, averaged one closed transaction a week for over 20 years in the real estate business, my entire adult life has been spent "putting it on the line" that demarcates the differences between success and failure, while at the same time marveling at what makes the two experiences different.

You could say that my motivation to figure out the process of success is like another person's motivation to master an instrument or play golf. I do it because I love to do it! So it is with a real sense of satisfaction and my sincerest wishes for your own success that I offer you this exceptional book; one that I know can immediately and forever change your life for the better.

JFW

Introduction

How to Use This Book

In featuring what are perhaps the three most important laws for success in life, this book presents two main themes for your consideration: first, about your process of achievement; and second, about your mindset for success. With 21 chapters that are each at the same time thorough but brief, the book is short enough to read in just one sitting yet deserving of any additional time you may need to fully contemplate the truly life changing information it contains.

The manuscript is divided into five basic sections. When first reading the book, follow that format from front to back for best overall comprehension. Thereafter, upon reading it again, you should find it easy to navigate from one concept to another in any direction you see fit. As you progress through the material, customize your copy of the book into a personal resource for success. Circle the quotations that jump out at you, and chronicle the notes you take in the open area provided at the very back.

As a book, *The Third Law of Success* is meant for anyone who wants to tap more of his or her potential to succeed in life.

Indeed, it is intended to benefit any person of any experience in any set of circumstances. That you can live in abundance while realizing more of your hopes and dreams is the point. Making that personalized vision real in your life is the objective. And you can do so by challenging yourself to bring the information you find on these pages to life in your daily experience of living…

Here's to your success!

"When you know what you want,
take action in that way, and
are open to opportunity...

...amazing is what happens!"

I.

The Nature of Success

"Words must be translated into action for success to occur."

1.

Quoting Success

The desire to succeed in life has been a driving factor for people around the world ever since man first walked the earth. Initially being more about basic survival—food, clothing, shelter, key customs and practices—information deemed vital was passed down from generation to generation by word of mouth to ensure that traditionally valued success techniques were not lost. With the onset of recorded history, however, the idea of what success means slowly began to evolve and broaden through the crosscultural comparison and discussion of ever more documented information on the subject. And as time marched on, mankind's breadth of knowledge and, with it, fascination concerning just what constitutes the nature of success continued to grow...

Gradually it became more apparent to more people that there were quantifiable and attainable upgrades to be gained when it comes to the process that leads to success in life; and not just regarding the basics but applicable in any direction imaginable. Consequently, as the dual objectives of "more" and "better" increased in people's minds, the idea of what success is became not only about survival but also about *quality* of survival. Ever since, men and women have been trying to unlock closed doors and uncover hidden secrets that shed new light not only on the actual experience of success but also on how best to achieve it.

As a result, down through the ages many prominent and accomplished individuals from all walks of life have offered their personal thoughts on what success might mean. From a classic perspective, for example, and certainly having withstood the test of time, it was the sage Greek philosopher Aristotle—student of Plato and teacher of Alexander the Great—who well over 2,000 years ago said,

> *"He who stops learning*
> *stops succeeding."*

Or in fast forwarding to the turn of the 20th century—a truly epic time of sweeping and world-altering technological, industrial, and cultural change—the American inventor-businessman about whom legend states needed 10,000 attempts to successfully invent the light bulb, Thomas Alva Edison, felt that…

> *"The first requisite for success is the ability to*
> *apply your physical and mental energies*
> *to one problem incessantly…"*

His fellow icons of the day—names like Carnegie, Vanderbilt, Bell, or the Wright brothers—sometimes spoke of their own individual roads to success (and ultimately great wealth) with a public eager to apply their notably fundamental yet life changing techniques. Henry Ford, for instance, openly shared his simple "secret" for personal success:

> *"Success is found in not quitting.*
> *Failure is the path of least persistence."*

Several decades later, when considering the many ups and downs of his long career in public service—indeed through two world wars—then former British Prime Minister Winston Churchill unabashedly proclaimed,

> *"Success consists of going*
> *from failure to failure*
> *without loss of enthusiasm."*

Alternatively, in clearly articulating what the experience of success can mean in life, consider what Earl Nightingale, the late, great motivational speaker, achievement coach, and author on success, had to say:

> *"Success is the progressive*
> *realization of a worthy ideal."*

And sometimes the arts point the way toward success... Take the insightful words of three time Academy Award winning actress Ingrid Bergman. She truly experienced the highs and lows of a rich and full life, all in the public eye, and once quite wisely compared the sometimes different but often interrelated states of success and happiness in life:

"Success is getting what you want;
happiness is wanting what you get."

Or, having put their inspired thoughts about the true essentials of great living to music, reflect on the beautiful and poetic lyrics of Beatles John Lennon and Paul McCartney:

"All you need is love, love.
Love is all you need."

And just for the fun of it, enjoy the innuendo-laden and often humorously insulting wit of the ever popular old-time Hollywood comedian Groucho Marx:

"The secret in life is
honesty and fair dealing.

If you can fake that,
you've got it made."

Then there is titan of technology Bill Gates' rueful critique on success that warns us there are no guarantees and the experience can be fleeting:

"Success is a lousy teacher...

*It seduces smart people
into thinking they can't lose."*

Certainly, there are many other possible descriptions for what success might mean to different individuals. And you likely have your own version(s), too. For my part, though, one way I generally define the concept of success in my own life is the opportunity to pursue and achieve my goals while I enjoy the process; in short, to both do well and be well. And the following suggestion is an excellent tip that I often personally rely on when wanting to ensure myself a reliable process of achievement:

*Day by day; step by step;
first things first.*

*"The only failure is
the failure to learn."*

2.

Three Secrets of Failure

Certainly, quotes from historical and current life leaders can help to pull back the curtain on the sometimes veiled secrets of success in life. In contrast however, there is not much mystery surrounding the typical secrets of failure that often vie to hold you back. Although many common pitfalls can beset you along the road to success, the following is a leading example that can block your path:

Trying to Do Everything

Just look at how impractical it is. There simply is not enough time to go around for all the different things you could possibly be doing. It is, of course, a basic fact of life that your time is limited. Consequently, the practice of going in far too many directions greatly diminishes your ability to succeed within the finite time frame available. Think about it logically:

You can't do everything.
When would you do it?

Remember that a jack-of-all-trades is likely the master of none. Unfortunately, by taking on too many tasks you effectively dilute your ability to succeed on your highest level. Therefore, in order to experience your very best of success, be careful to spend the precious time of your one-and-only life in ways that are supportive of your very top priorities. For everything else that comes up...

Think delegate or delete.

In addition to trying to do everything, consider the second typical tendency that people often opt in to in an unrealistic attempt to ensure their success. Being that it can readily become a compulsive type of behavior however, it is a mode of operation that can be particularly self-defeating to people who want to achieve their best:

Trying to Be Perfect

If generally true in your life (as it sometimes is in mine), this approach will undermine your efforts to succeed because true perfection is rarely attainable and usually not at all necessary. Indeed, when contemplating the nature of success there is a more viable approach to consider than seeking perfection because, from a functional standpoint,

Success isn't about perfection,
but rather progression.

Taking specific aim at the costly concept of trying to be perfect in the world of business, Meg Whitman—as President and CEO, first of eBay and then Hewlett-Packard—states in *The Power of Many*, her book about how to succeed in a major corporation without ethical compromise:

"Perfect is the enemy
of good enough."

What happens in such instances is, in trying to get everything perfectly set—which, philosophically perhaps, is an admirable goal—you do not move forward at a pace that the practicalities of success in business demand. In other words, getting things right does not necessarily have to mean making them perfect. The question to ask is whether what you have done is adequate to support the next step. If yes, move on. It is a practical and valuable approach toward success that I once heard put in a highly illustrative way from online marketing expert and coach Alex Mandossian. When it comes to getting things successfully done in business, he adamantly recommends…

"Sloppy success
over perfect mediocrity."

And as if neither trying to be perfect nor trying to do everything is enough, there is yet another popular inhibitor of success (and yet another challenge I often face in my own life) that can loom up to effectively hold you in check:

Trying to Please Everyone

This approach toward success can be quite exasperating to the would-be "pleaser" because the need to do it does not in fact mean that the subjects of your attention will be or even can be pleased. Upon thinking this tendency through you can see just how futile it is...

First of all, the sheer volume of people you may have to please in combination with their broad diversity as individuals effectively renders the idea of pleasing everyone to be a practical impossibility; statistically speaking, even pleasing half of the people half of the time would be a massive success. Secondly, and perhaps the real disadvantage of trying to please everyone, you put yourself in the difficult position of actually trying to do so, which therefore has the effect of rippling through the rest of your affairs in ways for which you must compensate accordingly.

And when you really look close at the high levels of anxiousness, frustration, and disappointment that occur with people pleasers who fail to please, you ultimately come to realize that, as with each of the self taxes in life, they actually are doing it to themselves. Or as said by respected life coach Anthony Robbins, who has helped people around the world to be their best...

"Nothing in life has any meaning
except the meaning you give it."

So cut yourself a break. The point of living is neither to do the most, nor to achieve perfection, nor to have everyone be delighted with you. Do not mistake such things for excellence but instead recognize them as impediments to that end. Based on the limitless possibilities of life, we all have (and need) much more leeway than that. Thus, when considering what the needed factors are to ensure what works best, call to mind that time-honored saying about people and their various approaches to success:

"Different strokes for different folks."

"Success lies in the mind of the beholder."

3.

A Question of Success

What is your definition of success...? Is it something you often think about? Can you readily and succinctly describe it to others? And how do you feel about it? Does your definition for success inspire you to become the person you truly can become? Do you find that it challenges you in ways that motivate you to give your very best? And finally, is it really achievable? Do you consistently apply your definition of success in your day to day process of living?

And what if you often think that success is not likely, at least not for you? What if you tend to doubt your ability to succeed? Might you hold yourself back because you are somehow mystified by your capacity for success, or because you are unclear in your mind about how to succeed? Could it be that your actual standards for success are unrealistic in ways that make it difficult to live up to your potential? Is it possible that, perhaps without knowing it, you prioritize avoiding failure over achieving success?

Those are just some of the many questions you can ask yourself when it comes to the subject of success in your life. And, when focusing on your own personal experience, it is really only you who can answer them. Although, just like for everyone else, due to the phenomenon of change in life at least one thing is certain:

What constitutes success will be different for you at different points in your life.

Perhaps a first car, graduating from school, a new home, or a pleasant retirement; or maybe a goal achieved, a project completed, or simply a certain milestone met...

For most people, a main measure of personal success is based on the quality of their relationships with family and friends. Or for some it is the depth of spiritual fulfillment in their lives. For others, an enriching road to personal success is found simply by helping others. And when it comes to one's work, although a dependable income and building wealth are often the main objectives, for many people professional success is not just about making money, but also about job satisfaction and career accomplishment.

In reality, any specific answers to the questions of success are not going to be the same from person to person. Being that we are individuals, we each have our own individual ways in which we define and measure our success, although we all do so both in qualities and quantities. Hence these familiar words often given in a celebratory toast:

*"Here's to health,
wealth, and happiness."*

Of course, when looking at success from a process point of view, it is often possible to identify an actual string of events progressing in a specific direction. But when you think about it in relation to the mental side of things, success is at the same time also a nonlinear yet specific state of consciousness; meaning, a subjective but nevertheless certain way of looking at things. In light of both of those examples, here are two classic definitions of the concept:

Success is a journey.

&

Success is a frame of mind.

Concise and simple versions both, yet definitions that elicit thought provoking questions about just exactly what kind of journey and what specific frame of mind might be involved. Again, such questions are for each person to answer because, if anything, success is a highly personal matter.

Still, even though it is up to each individual person to develop his or her own individual formula for success, any effective personal approach toward success must be based upon the fact that, as human beings...

Certain natural laws and bedrock principles exist that are true for all people.

Therefore, beyond any one exact definition of the word, what are the major, underlying factors that lead to success? Which fundamental laws must be understood and observed, and what basic principles must be embraced and applied by anyone who seeks to heighten the experience of success in his or her life?

In answer to those questions a host of descriptions, models, and steps have been articulated by thought leaders and luminaries from ancient times to modern day; all together which offer a wide variety of advice on how to make success happen in life. But none of those suggestions change the reality that, even though you naturally possess huge potential for success, the act of shaping your real life experiences into the fact of success is wholly on you.

In truth, that is what governing yourself well is all about – taking responsibility for the way you do things to get what you want out of life. In other words,

Success in life is not something you are given, it is something you achieve.

And that fact, once again, raises the all-important yet sometimes confusing question of just how it is best done.

Fortunately, though, out of the broad mix of information available on the subject of success in life there emerge three primary and powerful laws that generally apply to everyone – one known to many; one known to some; and one known to few.

Individually, each of the three great laws is vital to your experience of success in life. However, in working them together the three laws allow you to leverage and thus upgrade your approach toward success in ways you likely could not otherwise achieve. Consequently, to fully understand the key working concepts behind each law and to therefore better learn how all three best can work in concert, it is instructive to break them down into their respective and underlying parts...

II.

The First Law of Success

"Working to become the person you truly want to become is far less difficult than actually living without becoming that person."

4.

The Law of Action

There may not be a precise and accurate way to measure and therefore rank what are perhaps the three most important laws of success in life. The one likely considered by most people to be the first great law, however, is aptly described that way because, being the most commonly and overtly practiced of the laws governing the process of human achievement, it is the most well known:

The Law of Action

Down through history many noted scholars, leaders, teachers, and coaches have chimed in on what they believe to be the exact workings of this first great law of success. Not at all complicated in concept, there nevertheless exists a broad amount of information on the subject. With the idea of keeping it simple when contemplating this law however, recall what are said to be English philosopher and mathematician (and formulator of the universal laws of gravity, no less!) Sir Isaac Newton's most famous words...

*"What goes up must
come down."*

This first great law of success is traditionally associated with one of Newton's laws of motion that people around the world are generally familiar with, but that is perhaps more commonly known as the physical principle of cause-and-effect, that states:

*"For every action there is an
equal and opposite reaction."*

Essentially being based on the ways in which energy, force, and motion occur and interact at any moment, the law of action could logically also be called the law of physics. As such, this fundamental law exerts a major and significant influence over your day to day experience of living.

In human terms, the key to invoking the law of action is effort – that is, the expenditure of mental and/or physical energy to accomplish something. Indeed, on a personal level effort is the driving force behind this law because without effort action does not occur; which in turn evokes the key question implied when taking action:

What do I do?

Although simple to ask, it is a question that is not always easily answered. If you are to provide the type and amount of effort required to succeed, just remember that deeds are better than words. Accordingly, the following two classic expressions embody this first great law:

"You reap what you sow."

&

"No rules for success will work if you don't."

The all-important practice of action is application: persistently applying yourself to a specific task. However, since people tend to take action based on what they think they are going to get in exchange for their effort, it is often mistakenly thought that the law of action is principally about getting results. In contemplating the nature of action, though, it is not only what you do that counts but how you do it. Meaning, notwithstanding the unexpected effects of course-altering intangibles, your results in life are essentially the byproduct of your process. Obviously therefore, the way in which you apply yourself greatly influences what you get. Bearing that in mind from the perspective of action, one description of success might be:

*Working effectively to achieve
your goals and objectives.*

Certainly the relationship between action and success seems self evident: it is logical that without the former you do not have the latter. For example, Mark Twain—author, philosopher, and king of the commonsense quip—once commented:

*"The dictionary is the only place
where success comes before work."*

And because most people do easily grasp how the principle of cause-and-effect works in life, the law of action is surely the most commonly understood and rigorously applied of the main laws that govern the process of achievement. Instinctively, people everywhere jump right into action if not knowing then at least trusting that, if they do the work, their hoped for results can be and indeed will be achieved; which makes this first great law of major importance to the experience of success.

In a purely physical sense action is what makes things happen in life; and so the question to be answered regarding your success is how to best orchestrate the actions you undertake. As with most things, different people take different approaches toward that process. And that makes sense because, in order to experience the greatest effect of success as an individual, it is up to each of us to find our own particular definition of what works...

*"Your level of self-limitation in life
is actually an expression of your
potential capacity for greatness."*

5.

Success Limitation

---

*"Self-limitation is an odd thing
because it requires your participation."*

With the aim of a highly effective process of achievement in mind, pretty much everyone would agree without much discussion to the contrary that the trait of human laziness may be one of the least viable tickets for success; although laziness is not to be confused with the necessary counterbalance to action of allowing yourself the rest and relaxation you need. In contrast to pure laziness, the general tendency to keep busy all the time—i.e., action for action's sake—is not likely to be the best approach toward success either. Or as denoted in the fitting words of one of America's founding fathers,

"Never confuse motion with action."

That was Benjamin Franklin's way of pointing out that people can easily get caught up in a cycle of doing things, but not the things that need doing. In that way circling, they put in both time and effort but are just, as the saying goes, *"punching the clock"*. Consequently, they are not that effective in expanding their success. Simply put, people sometimes show up but do not step up. Perhaps passable tactics for just getting by in life, but in regularly not giving their best, they do not regularly achieve it. This is why, when it comes to observing the law of action, it is important to realize that you are not just a person who goes about doing things but that...

You are an achiever.

Once again, it is instructive to look back through time to the fundamental yet still much discussed teachings of Aristotle, who believed that...

"Excellence...is a habit."

Well, in using the same argument in reverse, lack of excellence, or success, could be a habit, too. And upon examination it is understandable how the underwhelming course of motion over action could become habitual. After all, a habit is simply a learned behavior that when repeated often enough becomes automatic. Therefore, if you are not vigilant to the possibility that you may not be "pedaling", over time the habit of coasting can be formed. And although some people seem to make what they do look easy, the process of high achievement does in fact take work for everyone. And so, when contemplating the level of your success, remember…

You can't coast uphill.

And it is very true. If you do not put in the specific effort needed to climb your own personal "mountain", achieving your greatest success is not the best bet. Frankly, consistently failing to deliver the necessary amounts of time and effort required to accomplish your goals and objectives is one of the chief reasons why you must put up with the dissatisfaction of holding yourself back. In addressing that point, take to heart the enduring words of all-time great basketball coach (and equally great life coach) John Wooden:

"Success is peace of mind…in knowing you did your best."

Beyond the obvious self-limitation of under effort, the urge for quick success, along with its easily enticing companion the proverbial shortcut, can loom up without much warning to block the full expression of action in your life. To avoid those temptations, it is prudent to observe the following truth when thinking about the experience of successful living:

"It's not that the grass is greener on the other side of the fence that matters, but that it's better tended."

Of course, what this means is that, for a better chance at achieving success and happiness in life, you had better get to work tending your own garden. It is very easy to look at where you are not, or to contemplate what you do not have, and to therefore justify grabbing for what seemingly look like the quickest and easiest solutions to the challenges you face.

I once read the account of a pioneer family traveling by covered wagon across the western territories of young America. Having lingered too long in the bountiful plains through the summer months, they arrived at the foot of an imposing mountain range in the late autumn of that travel season. In seeking to find a rumored shortcut directly over the mountains and, thus, save many weeks of travel on the already mapped route that skirted around the range, they found themselves unexpectedly and unpreparedly snowed in with no means of escape. After having endured several months of harsh winter weather and near starvation, the spring thaw eventually enabled them to backtrack to their original jumping off point from the regular trail. Upon ultimately arriving at their final destination nearly half a year later than the trip normally should have taken, a young woman who had survived the journey offered her simple but sincere advice—definitely learned the hard way—to any pioneer families that might follow:

"Don't take short cuts,
and hurry along your way."

Old school perhaps, but an excellent basic recipe for success, nonetheless. And, as it was then, it is still very good advice today. In looking back at the events of your life, surely there must have been a time or two when you would have been better served by such a down-home and direct approach toward some quick fix, yet regrettable course of action you undertook...

*"Be grateful for your challenges,
since through them you grow."*

6.

Über Action

While some people opt to coast through their lives on the lookout for shortcuts, other people dedicate themselves to the opposite track of working the most. In terms of the law of action however, though very likely to involve hard work, the experience of success is not always about working harder, or more. At some point, toiling constantly to reach your goal actually can slow you down or even lead you away from what your truest experience of success might most fully comprise....happiness. A fact to which any hard driving person who has experienced the phenomenon of personal burnout can attest.

Take for example the career story of an ambitious young businessman whose goal is to rise from the company mailroom to the corporate boardroom. Over the span of his career he is completely dedicated to his task and, forsaking many other pursuits, he works extremely hard. He stops at virtually nothing along the way and, upon one day being named CEO, he ultimately succeeds in reaching his longtime goal. During the man's impressive professional rise, however, he becomes an alienated workaholic who criticizes his coworkers and counterparts when they do not keep pace. And along the way, in not paying enough attention to his private life, he experiences two marriages that end in divorce, estranged relationships with his three children, high levels of emotional agitation, and a general state of poor physical health that eventually causes him to have a career ending heart attack.

Although not the path chosen by most people, such a relentless yet one-dimensional approach to success is not unheard of. Even though he did achieve his overall career objective of rising to the top, our corporate warrior simultaneously churned up a tremendously negative wake in his path; not just professionally but personally, as well. In his case, the man certainly could have benefitted from another exceptional piece of advice from the legendary John Wooden:

*"Don't let making a living
prevent you from
making a life."*

It turns out that we, as human beings, have the capacity to max ourselves out on the job and thus suffer from what is, essentially, over work. It is something like the effects of sleep deprivation in that, even though you do not like the constant fatigue and tiredness, you actually can get used to it. And if a habit takes hold, you just keep on going... Society in some ways even supports this approach, lauding the extremely hard worker who does not only take action, but who takes "über" action – the type of person who consistently does whatever it takes, for however long it takes; the person who seems to never back off.

And, as cited earlier, such über-taskers often do deliver big results, although the price in personal terms can be quite dear. Those who are prone to this type of action seem to lose touch with what is usually, at least for most people, the overall objective of living: not to be superhuman but to be a super human. Nevertheless, we can become so single-minded in our efforts to get from where we are to where we want to be that we end up forgetting (or ignoring) the real emotional, mental, and physical needs we have along the way to, as the familiar saying goes,

"Stop and smell the roses."

Sure, in order to accomplish your career (or other) goals, you oftentimes have to simply "stick it out" regarding the work you do. When it comes to getting the things done that need to be done, sometimes that is exactly what it takes; which points to the fact that it is not the act of working really hard where the potentially harmful challenge lies. Rather, it is the extended pattern over time of such an intense work ethic that can bring so many debilitating side effects into your life.

Just do not lose sight of what should be (but not always is) the obvious fact that you do not know what tomorrow will bring. People who ignore that reality or who convince themselves, perhaps through blind commitment to a certain objective, that they can trade what they have today for what they expect tomorrow, are playing a risky game because...

"Prediction is difficult;
especially about the future."

Those are the words of Danish physicist and philosopher Niels Bohr, who won the Nobel Prize in 1922 for his work contributing to the foundational understanding of atomic structure and quantum mechanics. Springing from a brilliant mind, his simple and witty statement is a profound depiction of the basic reality with which you live: that you neither know what, for sure, is going to occur nor whether you will, in fact, be around to see it happen. Most certainly, the journey of living changes daily and can be fleeting, which is why it is so important to appreciate and take advantage of the day-to-day aspect of life. Do not allow a lack of effort or the tendency toward idle motion or the allure of quick success or the compulsion to over work to keep you from experiencing a destiny of great living.

*"Each day of your life is a
once in a lifetime opportunity"*

7.

Living Destiny

Destiny. In defining that word, the dictionary gives several somewhat varying examples, but mostly in the sense of predetermination, inevitability, or fate; in other words, as something that is largely out of your control. But fortunately, in the open book of life your concept of destiny is something you can define for yourself because...

> *Destiny is not something*
> *dictated to you.*

Certainly, people do speak of wanting to "define" or, more often, "fulfill" their destiny, but they tend to talk about it as if it is something they are headed toward down the road and that they will "meet" off in the future. But if it is simply something you are to experience in the future, you limit your concept of destiny to an end result.

However, because of the significant power you wield to both create and react to the ongoing sequence of events in your life, destiny can be something much more significant than a destination. That is why I combine the word "living" with the word "destiny" when discussing the topic. As opposed to awaiting what is a fixed future destiny toward which life's journey inexorably pulls you,

> *"Living destiny" is about the conscious embrace of what you do today.*

Yet a common challenge exists for many people in terms of living their destiny. Although some can even picture in their mind the end result that they either want or believe they are fated to, for some reason far too many people do not prioritize and appreciate the day to day action steps representative of making such a mental picture a reality. By default they therefore diminish the power they have to achieve the things they want in life and, at the same time, derive less satisfaction (and thus less enjoyment) from their experience of living. Consequently, often in high frustration and suffering the aftereffect of regret, they continue to get whatever it is they get and are then left to wonder why. And that—because instant gratification appeals to a part of our basic nature as human beings—is precisely when people start looking for miracles...

Due to the human ability to conceive of a future, people have attempted to miraculously change how their lives would end up since the dawn of mankind. Playing on that tendency, the legends of time gone by are full of conjurers, magicians, wizards, and sorcerers who claimed to have translated the ancient philosophy of alchemy into the actual science of turning lead into gold; which was in essence both a metaphor in support of the experience of quick success in life and an accepted justification for seeking a future destiny of material wealth as the objective of a great living.

In his modern classic, *The Alchemist*, author Paulo Coelho contrasts a more life embracing scenario of destiny through his charming fable about following your dream in life. Set in a former age, it is a novel about a Spanish shepherd boy who risks his all to travel east across the vast, arid wilderness of northern Africa in pursuit of great riches he dreamt await him at the base of the three pyramids in Egypt. Though having endured hardship and unforeseen circumstances along the way, the young shepherd has the good fortune to meet a mysterious, wise man of the desert—the Alchemist—who teaches him a completely new approach toward the nature of success and happiness in life. At one point the shepherd specifically asks the Alchemist why so many men have failed in their attempts to turn lead into gold—perhaps really inquiring why they are not satisfied with their lives—and the Alchemist answers,

"They were looking only for gold...

They were seeking the treasure of their destiny, without wanting actually to live out the destiny."

The Alchemist taught the youthful traveler that the way he approached destiny in life was his to choose. And that, in listening to his heart and, in that light, making conscious choices each day about what sincerely matters to him, he could experience a better way of living; one that would provide great riches of many different kinds. Rather than continuing to deaden his life experience by seeking treasure off in the future, in raising his awareness of what was happening around him in the moment, the young Spaniard chose to treasure his actual process of living and, as a result, experience his own living destiny of happiness one day at a time.

Each of us has that very same possibility: to decide the destiny we each want to live; which means that you can, as well. And although you just might choose to do so, you do not have to trek across the wilds of North Africa to make it so. It works equally well from wherever you are because, one step at a time, you can get to anywhere from there... But you really do have to look at your life as an ongoing journey; one that only you can take and, it follows, one that only you can "make". And if along the way you allow yourself to let go and enjoy the ride, as you accomplish many great things in your life your final destination is much more likely to take care of itself in a way that you will surely treasure.

*"Today is the unit of your lifetime;
so goes today, so goes your lifetime."*

8.

Today Is The Day!

The Alchemist is a short but illuminating novel that illustrates how a person can journey through life looking for riches while missing the richness of the journey of living. But in describing the probable nature of success in life, the two ends of high achievement and great happiness are not mutually exclusive. Indeed, in breaking it down to its most basic components perhaps the fullest experience of success is one part getting where you want to go and another part enjoying the process of getting there. Still, people too often find the joy of living to be elusive. When it comes to the actual experience of both success and happiness in life they easily lose their way by not fully appreciating that...

Today is the day!

Even though the first law of success clearly calls for action in life, it is up to you to not let the demands of that process drown out your awareness of living. Toward that end, I often recite a popular and cleverly beautiful saying sometimes attributed to Eleanor Roosevelt but that, in varying forms, predates her:

"The past is history, the future is a mystery, and today is a gift...

That's why they call it the present."

Upon first hearing them many years ago those poetically moving words immediately rang true with me. In considering the depth of meaning that they suggest I began to explore a new and powerful way of looking at life. And eventually, in an inspired burst some years later, I wrote my own impassioned ode to the present:

"Today is the day! There is no yesterday. There is no tomorrow. Anything that ever happens will only ever happen when it is today. Worry about the past or the future can easily compromise the day you are actually living. Your sense of living can be forgotten as you look in your mind to what has happened or might happen on a different day. Appreciate what you have. And what you only ever have is today.

"Today is the day! In reality, the past and the future are mental concepts and, as such, they only ever happen in your mind. Use them to learn, to plan, and to dream. Do not allow them to use you, in that you waste your only real day, which is today. Make today the main focus of your mind. Know that if you want to change the world, you should change it today. And if you want to change your world, you should change your today.

"Today is the day! Do not miss it because once today is gone you can never get it back. Place your highest value on today. Energize yourself with the understanding that whatever you do will actually only be done while it is today. Be aware and alert today. Be open and creative today. Be curious and adventurous today. Be positive and encouraging today. Be useful and helpful today. Be fun today. Be happy today. Love today!

"Today is the day! It is your day and, therefore, it is up to you to make it a great day. Be clear about what you want today. Connect to your passion today. Recognize that opportunity is everywhere today. Do not hold yourself back today. Be the best you can be today. Know where you are going today. Act on your potential today. Count your

blessings today. Be grateful for today. And whatever you do, open the gift of today because....Today is the day!"

The preceding verse underscores the importance of living in the now, but also points to still another facet of action: urgency. Remember, you only can take action in any form when it is today. Therefore, in heeding the first law of success while minding your experience of happiness in life, perhaps the immediate first steps you should take are to wake up and enjoy the day you are living. That is why I often tell people,

"Life is todaily."

Although not found in any dictionary, the word *"todaily"* is my term for something that is *"occurring today, each and every today."* Therefore, the saying *"life is todaily"* describes the basic reality that the ongoing experience of living only happens in the now. And in part, the message behind the fact that life occurs in the present moment is, again, that you must take action today, not someday; which for many people is simply another word for never.

Of course, you already know this. However, like just about everyone else, when the multiple and never-ending distractions of life keep popping up and clogging your radar, you sometimes tend to forget. Consequently, relying solely on action may not be enough for you to realize your fullest measure of success in life. Instead, to be more effective within your process of achievement, the law of action works much better in conjunction with a second great law for success; a powerful law that brings a purposeful and more connected approach toward your todaily efforts to succeed...

III.

The Second Law of Success

*"You are meant to live
the life you dream about."*

9.

The Law of Attraction

Of particular importance in sparking the law of action, yet integral in its own right to the process of achievement in life, the next great law of success is referred to as the second law only for the purposes of organization and description within this book:

The Law of Attraction

Otherwise, it could be the first law of success because, when not observing it, people easily do fall into the trap, as Ben Franklin suggested, of mistaking motion for action. Due to a lack of meaning and direction in their lives, they too often pass their days stuck in a groove of success inhibiting routine. In that mode—forgetting that life is todaily—they unconsciously allow their time, which is their most limited and therefore most precious resource, to slip away day by day without really challenging themselves to live life to the fullest.

In an effort to help people further understand how it pertains to their lives, much defining work has been done on the concept of attraction in recent years. Accordingly, as with the law of action, there is a broad and diverse body of information available on the topic. Yet, in keeping with the short but sweet description accredited to him for the workings of gravity—"*what goes up must come down*"—in an attempt to just as simply and precisely describe this second great law of success it is reasonable to suggest that Isaac Newton might have said this:

"Focus on something attracts it back."

Although much talked about, attraction is possibly the most misunderstood and, therefore, misapplied law of success. At times touted as something new or even "new age", the law of attraction has always been one of the cornerstones to building a foundation of success in life. And it is based upon the mentally dominant principle of attention-and-experience, that says:

"Clear intention supports a course of action in that direction."

Characterized by the ways in which specific representations of desire, passion, and purpose work today to influence and affect what may occur someday in the future, the law of attraction could also be called the law of potential. In that sense, this second great law of success directly impacts what possibly *could* happen in your life. And the tremendously powerful effect it exerts over your actual experience of living is undeniable…

For any person, the key to invoking the law of attraction in life is clarity – how clear you are about what is most important to you. From a personal standpoint, the level of clarity you have is the driving force behind this law because high clarity activates the process of attraction; which, it follows, evokes the must answer question of attraction:

What do I want?

This is not just a surface question but rather one directed deep at your core. And it is necessary to specifically and accurately answer if you are to define the depth and breadth of clarity supportive of the action likely needed to succeed on a high level. Thus for many people this second great law of success is exemplified by the two following often-repeated sayings. First, the life changing message from Earl Nightingale's classic audio recording (and my favorite), *The Strangest Secret*:

"You become what you think about."

And second, the overriding yet simple theme from the insightful teachings of Napoleon Hill, perhaps the godfather of the modern self-improvement movement:

"Believe and achieve."

Essential to kick starting the process of attraction is the practice of specification: framing and visualizing in your mind what you truly want. But because in approaching this particular law much emphasis is placed on the exact thing(s) desired, the idea of attraction is commonly misunderstood to be about wishful thinking or even willpower. However, there is more to the concept of attraction than making a wish or strength of will...

Upon closer evaluation and, in particular, in relation to a functional process of achievement, it turns out that the conscious act of attracting an expressly implied result into your life—often known as manifestation—is not only about you wanting something, but also about you wanting to do something about it. As in the story of the young boy who was found furiously digging in a huge pile of horse manure... When asked why, he responded excitedly: *"With a pile that big, there's gotta be a pony under there somewhere!"*

Certainly a humorous account, but also one that illustrates what are two different aspects of the phenomenon of attraction; not just clarity, but also willingness. The boy absolutely knew what he wanted—his very own pony—and he was willing to do what it took to get it, even digging in you know what! And it is a telling tale that points to the reality of attraction as just one lane in the two-way street of achievement. If the process is to work well, for what you desire to come toward you, you must go toward what you desire. Thus my pointed saying,

"Commitment is not just stated,
but demonstrated."

Meaning that, within the process of achievement, attraction is not only about getting life to happen to you, but also about getting you to happen to life. Which is to say, if you sincerely do want a desired result to come into your life, once you have clearly envisioned it in your mind you will more willingly apply yourself in that direction. Accordingly, in accounting for the actual interworking between the law of action and the law of attraction, a popular definition of success would likely be:

Striving to live the life
you dream about.

*"Limitation decreases
as awareness increases."*

10.

Open Up to What's Possible

Although people everywhere tend to agree on the basic mechanics of action, some differing thought exists pertaining to the workings of attraction. And certainly there is room in the world for various interpretations of the concept, with each person of course being entitled to his or her opinion. Regarding the basis for my own thinking however, over the years the classroom of life has taught me—sometimes painfully—the following lesson about how best to look at things:

*It's better to
be open than right.*

It is good advice because an open mind is essential to an effective process of learning; and possessing a desire and ability to learn certainly is one of the keys to success in life. And like you, although I might have my individual definition of what it means, success matters to me. In that same vein—being open—I once saw a fun bumper sticker that said,

*"My karma just ran over
your dogma!"*

After a quick chuckle, what that statement implies to me is that, as living and (hopefully) evolving human beings, we should endeavor to get out of our own way and thus more fully open up to what is possible in our lives. There is not necessarily any one "right" way. That is why I often suggest to people…

*"Assumption is the mother
of self-limitation."*

So instead of taking too much for granted in your life or, worse, thinking you know it all, remind yourself that things may or may not be what you assume they are. Toward that end, challenge yourself to stay alert and open to what is actually occurring. And for the purposes of getting to the truth about how things do in fact work, make it a priority to maintain an inquiring mind. In that light, remember that for any person to effectively tap into the power of attraction within his or her process of achievement, it is helpful to separate fact from non fact… In again quoting the wry humor of Mark Twain:

*"Get your facts first, and then you
can distort them as you please."*

A turn of phrase said with a wink and a smile, yes. But it also suggests that those who are uncertain (or, perhaps, who are certain) as to how the law of attraction works might want to inquire further... Doing so is important because, not only *can* you,

*You naturally do
attract things into your life.*

This means the process of attraction is at work in your daily life even though you may not be aware of it. And it is a phenomenon that is experienced in an endless variety of ways, whether through life changing events or in simple everyday occurrences.

Certainly, you have had basic instances when a desire in the back of your mind comes into greater focus and ultimately pops up in your life as something real. Like, for example, when you need a new car and you happen to see a recently released model that catches your eye. Thereafter, almost as if in reminder of both your need and desire, you continue to spot more and more of that same model car around town. Eventually you happen to notice an enticing ad in the newspaper for that very vehicle and, voilà, you end up driving one yourself. In this example you could say that attraction works as a kind of awareness.

Or perhaps you have noticed upon arriving at a social gathering how people form into different groups. Associations first tend to occur based on level of familiarity, and second according to what is being discussed. But as the minutes pass, people tend to gravitate toward and away from one another based on the "vibe" they are feeling. The levels of enthusiasm and positivity versus negativity and passivity—each a form of energy—will often ultimately be what determines who ends up talking, or not talking, with whom. In this way attraction occurs essentially through a sense of feel.

The truth is that we each experience such fundamental working examples in our daily lives of how both our sense for energy and our awareness of energy are so very compelling. The ensuing question is if you pay attention to the specific process at work behind such scenarios, because it can become a directed technique. And if you can get a handle on a conscious practice of attraction—the act of being clear and consistent about what you want—you will significantly upgrade your experience of living by commanding much greater influence over what comes into your life, whether big or small and no matter what it might be.

But it can also downgrade your quality of life because the basic process of attraction works in any direction. Positive or negative, precise or vague, confident or doubtful; the process responds in accordance to the specific energy given. Furthermore, the process does not have an opinion or care about what kind of energy that may be; which is why *you* must be alert to the reciprocal relationship between thought and energy. And that interplay is based on the common fact in life that oftentimes...

Like energy attracts.

What that suggests from a technical perspective is that attraction occurs when the particular vibration of energy produced by a specific thought or emotion in your mind in some way tracks, or synchronizes, with similar vibrations of energy from sources on the plane of the physical world all around you. And that when such a pattern of synchronization is consistent, specific effects representative of what you have been thinking begin to take shape and/or show up in actual form in your life. As a result, even though not always apparent or immediately measureable, the momentum of attraction tends to build and, through the sum expression of many contributing variables, ultimately compound into a live-time version of the experience you seek.

If that sounds a bit complex, do not worry. Being able to fully and precisely articulate the concept of attraction is not the point. Fortunately, you do not need to explain it or even understand it in order for the process to work for you (or, unfortunately, against you). And neither do you need to know the specific action steps you should take for your intended success to occur. With attraction, that is not your role in the process. At its essence, harnessing the power of attraction in life only stipulates that your mind be a broadcasting beacon for your truest desires. So pay good attention to the quality of your thoughts because...

The universe is listening!

"When you truly show up,
so will the things you truly want."

11.

Attractive Coalescence

A central point often taught about attraction is that the universe is an infinitely abundant place that can readily provide you with most anything you desire in life. And when you look at just how amazingly vast and diverse the universe is, that has certainly got to be the case. However, the best way to actually access such universal abundance in their lives is not so obvious for most people. As for myself, when looking back at my experience with the process of achievement in life, I have learned over time to focus on whatever it is that actually works. And through 20 years of research, observation, and reflection on the subject I have identified a basic truth about the mechanics of attraction:

You are not only the transmitter,
but also the receiver.

This is to say that while the universe is listening, so are you. In clearly and precisely knowing what you want, you not only send an express message of vibrant energy out from yourself into the universe, so to speak, but just as importantly (or perhaps even more so) you also send the same message deep into your consciousness. As a result, both when looking outward at the world around you and in observing the inner depths of your own desire, you tune in to giving and receiving more of what is possible that might pertain to the specific objective you have in mind. And because you have consciously identified and featured in your mind's eye the specific want that you hold to be important, the following three things occur:

1) You better represent and, in that way, present a clear message of intent to the world about, which will then react to that energy in ways both seen and unseen.

2) You are more aware and, as a result, will specifically note and marshal more of the world's resources that come to bear on actualizing the subject in question.

3) You are more open and, thus, more likely to take the kind of direct mental and/or physical action that is supportive of making your objective quantifiably real.

This is the power of "attractive coalescence", or of the three facets of attraction (intention, awareness, oppenness) coming together to influence outcome in your life. Indeed, when you are crystal clear about what you want—

through the world's reaction to it, your heightened awareness of it, and your resultant behaviors toward it—the inward and outward message of intent that you both send and receive does, without a doubt, echo back to you in clearly tangible ways. In that manner you absolutely do attract things into your life.

Bottom line, if the particular message of intent that you both send and receive is an accurate representation of your truth, the energy you project and your mental frame of reference and, in turn, your resultant action steps each collaborate with the other in ways that help to align your world with your desired way of living. Or you simply could say…

*"Attractive coalescence is
attraction in action."*

Whether a rewarding career change or a more fulfilling personal relationship or the acquisition of something new—from the latest techno-gadget to your own jet—if you really want to attract it into your life, it is key that you generate and maintain the corresponding energy value to exchange for it. And it is through the interplay of clear intention (your projection of energy) and active awareness (your attention to possibility) and openness to action (your willingness to work) that you stimulate such a real life exchange. In this sense it is illustrative to say that one plus one plus one equals *more* than three. In other words, when the three facets of attraction interfunction in relation to something you truly want, more and more things begin to occur in your life that are representative of it.

And interestingly (and significantly) the law of attraction's basic principle of attention-and-experience—*clear intention supports a course of action in that direction*—works in close parallel and conjunction with the law of action's fundamental principle of cause-and-effect—*for every action there is an equal and opposite reaction.* When applied in concert, these two "active" and "attractive" principles work effectively to support and, therefore, advance your process of achievement.

On the practical level of daily life, the clearer and more open you are in relation to what you want, the more your personal vibe and manner will attract like energy for you to effectively shape and mold into an experience of living in that very light. Consequently, the odds of achieving what you are after go way up. Therefore, you also could say…

> ## *"Clarity is the primary actuator for attraction in action."*

What matters is not simply how bad or how much you want something to come into your life, but rather how truthful and clear you are with yourself about wanting it to do so in lieu of the other options you also have; which is a subtle yet major distinction. Just think of it in light of the tickling malapropism ascribed to Major League Baseball's Yogi Berra:

> ## *"If you don't know where you're going, you'll wind up someplace else."*

Most fundamentally, therefore, an effective process of achievement begins with true personal clarity about what you want. This is because accurately identifying what you most truly want is a vital and necessary factor in igniting the two-stroke engine of attraction and action within that process.

"You do what is most important to you."

12.

Whypower

Like so many people, you are a motivated and capable individual who wants to succeed. As such, your life in today's fast paced world often pulls you in many competing directions. And in trying to handle so many things, especially when feeling harried and overworked, you find yourself relying on your personal levels of self-discipline and willpower to stay on track. You know the drill: when you do not feel like doing something, yet you do it anyway. At some point along the way, though, as a kind of tension and thus resistance builds up in your mind, you become either frustrated about how things are going or downhearted about continuing on or, perhaps worse, simply apathetic about where you are; which are typical situations when self-discipline fails and willpower abandons you, and so you stop.

Interestingly, even though the words are not synonymous, the idea of willpower is often confused with the concept of self-discipline. The primary meaning of the root word "discipline" as defined in the dictionary is, *"Training to act in accordance with rules."* Therefore, the level of your "self-discipline" in life is typically a byproduct of how well you have trained yourself to perform up to a certain standard; which, although very important, nevertheless goes back to action, or the physical side of achievement.

In contrast, not at all like self-discipline, willpower is about the mental side of achievement. Once again citing the dictionary, the word "willpower" is defined as, *"Control of one's impulses and actions; or self-control."* And so even though willpower works well up to a point—it only being about your mental level of *"control"* over what you do but not about the *reason* you do it—for most people straight willpower has its limits, particularly when the daily pressures of living begin to mount. To put it simply, as it gives way you give up. Fortunately, there is another approach to driving yourself forward in life that is less taxing than the rigors of developing high self-discipline and more powerful than the practice of simple willpower:

Whypower

Different from both the concepts of self-discipline and willpower, instead of maintaining control over your actions through in-depth training and/or utter determination, whypower is based on tapping into and maintaining your heartfelt connection to the reason you do things. If the reason behind what you are doing is something genuinely important to you it generates passion, which is perhaps your greatest source of motivation in life. If you regularly connect to it, such passion—being an emotional reaction that is at the same time both a mental and physical reflection of the thing you want—provides a much more abundant and renewable source of "motivative" energy to drive you forward than mere willpower can; and it does so without all the effort and preparation that goes into developing a high level of selfdiscipline. That is why I say,

> *"The people who stay conscious*
> *of their why, win."*

Meaning, with a passionate reason for why you want something clearly fixed in your mind, through the process of attractive coalescence—the potent interplay of intention and awareness and openness—you stimulate and initiate a chain of events that in turn causes you to willingly both give and receive more of what is needed to stay on that specific track. In comparison, undeveloped discipline and pure force of will are too often not enough to keep you on course over an extended period, especially when the challenges you face in going forward seem most intense. And so, when urging them to be their best, I always ask people,

> *"What's your gap frame?"*

Concerning any particular aspect of your life—often a project or objective you are working on or toward—your gap frame is the time it takes between when you mentally fall off track and when you get back on track. In essence then, your gap frame is a measure of your effectiveness. And in terms of your process of achievement, it of course stands to reason that a short, or small, gap frame is an advantage over a big one. Thus, any effective answer to the question of how to shorten your gap frame is one that gains you such an advantage. And, once again, your ability to connect yourself to the passion behind what is most important to you is where the answer can most consistently be found.

And so both whypower, generally, and connection, specifically, are the two main factors in bridging the gap between continued performance and nonperformance. Just remember that your results in life are typically a byproduct of your process. And in considering the process of achieving in relation to the results achieved, you may want to bear in mind the following bit of classic advice pertaining to the law of action:

> ## "Nothing great is ever achieved without great effort."

When considering the law of action, those words remind us of one of the great truths of high achievement: that you have got to do the work. But also remember that your continued success does not solely depend on working ever harder. Again, with that approach you will eventually "flame out". And so, to help you maintain your ongoing quest for success, be certain to "plus" the physical and mental investments you make with this insightful piece of companion advice that you can see encompasses basic elements of the law of action and the law of attraction, both:

> ## "No great effort is ever sustained without great passion."

Simple in concept, whypower then (and by extension, attraction) is about passion. Certainly not rocket science, but definitely rocket fuel. Powered by passion, anything you are capable of can be accomplished; and you are capable of so very much. Therefore, in going forward in life clearly align your actions with your intentions. Meaning, take care to connect the things you actually do with the things you truly want. In so doing, you will…

Power your progression
with your why.

"Getting to your truth opens you up to reality, which is where things happen..."

13.

The Seminal Question

Although the universe—in this sense, every aspect of the world in which you live—does provide you with the means for success, in reality your actual success is not up to the universe, it is up to you. You are the active ingredient. In other words, if you are going to interact with the world around you in a way that causes more of what you would like to occur in your life to indeed happen, then you are the one who must gain clarity surrounding what you want, and who then must maintain your connection to it. Thoroughly and consistently do those two things, and virtually no dream is too big.

I once overheard the grandparents of a 10 year old boy ask him what it was he wanted to do when he grew up, and he quickly answered with enthusiasm: "*Own a baseball team!*" It is amazing how clearly children can envision what they want; they seem to naturally possess vivid feelings about it. The only question as they grow up becomes whether or not the many vagaries of life will mount up to dim the light of that passion to the point of effectively blocking their path in the direction of their dreams.

Wonderfully, as a child you, too, may have seen the potential for your success as something quite natural. As an adult, in contrast, you likely have learned that success in living the life you dream about can be very elusive. Unfortunately, the very experience of living, through its inevitable disappointments and struggles, may have conditioned you to think small and to play it safe and, too often, to settle for whatever you get. That is why I like the clever and ever success-minded thinking of famous New York businessman Donald Trump, who advises:

"Since you're going to be thinking anyway, you might as well think big!"

And it is true; at any moment you can go from small thinking to thinking big and, thus, begin to break your pattern of self-limiting behavior. However to leverage the advantage of thinking big into the act of success, that "big" thing you want must be maintained as one of your top priorities. And you can do that by developing an ongoing relationship with the seminal question of life:

"What is it you want?"

With the seminal question in fact being the original, basic question that everything comes back to within your personal process of achievement in life, the answers it evokes work to influence the very course of events throughout your experience of living. Consequently, it is of great importance to make it your habit to ask the question of what it is you want whenever you come upon one of the unmarked crossroads of life. At those times the ability to summon clear and truthful answers about what is most important to you in your heart will bring the power of your passion to the forefront and, consequently, help you to overcome the many obstacles that seem to block your way.

In yet another passage from *The Alchemist*, the shepherd boy asks, *"Why do we have to listen to our hearts?"* And the Alchemist answers, *"Because, wherever your heart is, that is where you'll find your treasure."* And then, in admitting to a deep fear of failure, the young seeker tells the desert master, *"My heart is afraid that it will have to suffer."* To which the Alchemist responds, *"Tell your heart that the fear of suffering is worse than suffering itself. And that no heart has ever suffered when it goes in search of its dreams."*

The above story emphasizes the importance of being clear about what you want in your life for the basic reason that you will be more effective in dealing with the emotion of fear. And that is of great significance because, it being an evolved survival tool that is meant to protect you from perceived danger by holding you back, the feeling of fear is one of the biggest obstacles you will ever face on your path to success.

Essentially, there are only two types of fear: the kind you experience in response to a real danger; and that which is only in your head. And when the latter happens, you are sometimes still prone to hold yourself back and, thus, disrupt your process of achievement – all for no good reason. That is why the following acronym is a great reminder about much of the fear that you feel in your life:

F. E. A. R. – False Evidence Appearing Real.

And it is true, I think, that much of the fear we experience is in fact unfounded; which is why it is so important to regularly ask yourself the seminal question, "What is it you want?" Because when you are clear about what you want most in life, you can tap the whypower needed to help you move past the "faux fear" in your head and, thus, stay far more on track.

Again, even though you might not see it or may not believe it, you possess a huge capacity to achieve; as a human being, you are literally wired for it. And you can develop that innate capacity for achievement into a practical ability for achievement. But to do so you must heed certain fundamental laws and essential principles that govern the process of achieving your best.

Both the law of attraction (having to do with potential and, it follows, clarity about what drives you) and the law of action (dealing with physics and, therefore, the effort you give) are two such keys for unlocking the experience of success in your life. Respectively, they can be refined down to these primary issues:

What you want.

&

What you do.

And it is certainly true that people everywhere typically focus much of their effort to succeed in those two ways when aiming for quantifiable results. In practice, however, neither the law of action nor the law of attraction typically returns the fullest measure of success when observed alone. In truth, each law greatly relies on the other law when it comes to gaining a more effective process of achievement. When orchestrated together these first two great laws of success enable you to better harness the inherent power you possess to "go big" in your life.

IV.

The Third Law of Success

"Change makes the world go around.
Embracing change makes it go forward."

14.

The Law of Acceleration

In following the first two classic laws of success—the laws of action and attraction—you set the stage to accomplish and enjoy many good things in your life. Yet, if you are to get the most out of your process of achievement, in addition to the law of action and the law of attraction, there exists a third great law of success. If consciously observed, it will cause a major and beneficial shift in your approach toward life and, as a result, energize your experience of living:

The Law of Acceleration

This law is not at all well known and, as a result, not nearly so commonly or overtly applied by people searching for success in their lives. And like the law of attraction it too could justifiably come before the law of action. This is because, in large part, the law of acceleration has to do with mindset, and a proper mindset is what sets the stage for effective action. In distilling this third law of success down to its essence, perhaps Newton might have suggested this for the concept of acceleration:

"Constant change equals
ever present opportunity."

That understanding is too often the missing piece within one's process of achievement. And when combined with the laws of action and attraction it will bring a much heightened sense of success into your day-to-day experience of living. Certainly, when fully comprehended and actively applied, the law of acceleration has the power to be a true game changer in most any aspect of your life. And it is based upon the universally prevalent but largely unfamiliar principle of transformation-and-possibility, which observes...

"All change is opportunity manifesting
itself in a new direction."

It could also be called the law of benefit because this law defines the ways in which change, possibility, and awareness act upon and interact with one another to enhance the level and nature of success you identify and experience in the present moment; which, if you think about it, is the only place opportunity can be found. Accordingly, and if observed in full, this remarkable law opens your eyes to a new way of looking at life and, in resultantly modifying your behavior toward opportunity, upgrades the way you live it.

As an individual, the key to invoking the law of acceleration is interpretation; meaning in this sense, how you define your world relative to the phenomenon of opportunity. And the ability to translate the events of life from an opportunity perspective—the driving force behind this law—depends on how you look at things; which logically evokes the baseline question when seeking to accelerate your experience of success:

What do I see?

This question is posed not only to ask what you observe physically, but also to inquire what you perceive mentally; to interpret both the objective and the subjective circumstances you encounter from the standpoint of opportunity. Therefore, it is a question that must be asked *and* answered with a curious and open mind if you are to clearly view the never-ending possibilities of life through the lens of opportunity. With that in mind, the following expressions represent this third great law:

*"He who is good with a hammer
sees everything as a nail."*

&

*"In the middle of difficulty
lies opportunity."*

The practice central to accelerating your daily experience of success is orientation: embracing and exploring the phenomenon of opportunity in your life. This can be done effectively in any scenario or situation in which you find yourself by asking yourself the question-of-opportunity:

Where's the opportunity?

Unfortunately, most people believe that opportunity is a rare thing and, as such, that it only happens occasionally; which is essentially a kind of scarcity thinking that subtly fosters a negative and self-limiting mindset that too often preempts such opportunity-minded inquiry. Yet in thinking about the nature of opportunity, just the reverse is true.

The main concern relative to opportunity is not whether it readily exists, but whether it is readily recognized; a concept that, although rarely taught, is a crucial insight into what is a direct catalyst for personal success: the development of an opportunity orientation toward your process of living. Thus, when it comes to the law of acceleration an apt definition of success is...

Seeing opportunity in any situation.

Indeed an illuminating description that casts new light on what it takes to succeed in life. And as you contemplate that fact in relation to your own journey of living, consider the often quoted and profound words of Napoleon Hill in his ever popular book about success, *Think and Grow Rich*:

"Opportunity often comes disguised in the form of misfortune or temporary defeat...

Every adversity, every failure, and every heartache carries with it the seed of an equivalent or a greater benefit."

As you will see, this is undeniably true. No matter what events transpire in life, at a minimum there is always the fundamental opportunity to learn; the basic opportunity to adapt; the always present opportunity to grow.

"*Opportunity is three-dimensional.*

It occurs at any time,
in any form, in any place."

15.

Natural Progression

Once again, the foundation upon which the law of acceleration rests is the universally applicable principle of transformation-and-possibility; a primary yet relatively unknown principle for success that, although previously noted, bears repeating:

"All change is opportunity manifesting itself in a new direction."

In turn, the principle of transformation-and-possibility is based upon the all affecting and ever occurring process of natural progression, which is the organic transmutation of energy into opportunity in life. Importantly, how you function in relation to that specific process has a major effect on the level, or amount, of success you experience from day to day because it depicts what are, in essence, the actual mechanics of abundance in life. Therefore, it is of key importance to understand how the process works and, ultimately, how it applies to you…

Natural Progression

At their most fundamental basis, all things in the universe are composed of pure energy. The common composition of all things interconnects everything on that basic level; which means that, whether seen or unseen on the plane of human perception, the interaction of all things is happening in some way. Consequently, the universal environment is one of varied and constant change. Constant change, in turn, ceaselessly works to ensure that the universe, and therefore your world, is one of infinite possibility, or all possibility; not in the sense that anything is possible, but rather in that the range of what is possible is infinite in scope.

It is the above process of natural progression that creates the physical reality of always occurring possibility within which all human beings exist. And when you as an individual, through the filter of your awareness—that is, by paying attention—consciously open up to and align yourself with the natural energy-to-possibility progression of existence, the process becomes an inexhaustible source, or field, of ever present opportunity for you in your life.

Again, this means that the most important issue with opportunity is not if it exists but whether or not it is recognized; being the part that is up to you. Thus, the clearer you are about what you truly want and the more open you are to what is really happening and the more you explore what might in fact be possible, the more latent, or always present, opportunity you will see in your daily experience of living. In other words, the world naturally functions in a way that provides for opportunity to be found in any situation you encounter. You could therefore say...

"Regarding opportunity, all you must do is wake up to it!"

Take, for instance, the man on a long business trip who is dog-tired from traveling but, due to an unusually sudden change in the weather, must wait out an overnight delay for his flight home. While dining alone in a strange city yet again, instead of closing himself off, he stays open to the possibility of interacting with the people around him. As a result, he has the opportunity to meet a highly respected and interestingly unique person (also weather-bound) with whom, as it turns out, he goes on to enjoy not only an immensely profitable business relationship but also a rewarding and lifelong friendship.

Or consider the woman doing research on a two year project in the medical field whose very best efforts fail resoundingly to formulate an improved treatment for people who struggle with painful stomach ulcers. Even though she feels physically drained and emotionally down about all the time and effort she seems to have lost, she opens up to what might still be possible by asking herself, "*Where's the opportunity?*" That question prompts her to reevaluate in a different light all the data she has painstakingly amassed. And within that very body of information she unexpectedly discovers a new and effective medication for sufferers of a completely unrelated ailment.

Amazingly, the same underlying process can be true for you, too. Because the world and your existence in it are both in a state of continuous change, the prismatic effect of possibility is invariably occurring all around you. With the reality being neither simple black and white nor the variation of gray scale, the awe-inspiring truth is that...

Life is rainbow!

What this means is that the experience of living quite naturally provides you with a never ending stream of new possibilities that represent endlessly varying directions you can take. Wondrously, the permutations of change—the phenomenon central to the process of natural progression in which change itself in turn effects more change—ensure this to be true. If you live in tune with that process you can always rest assured that, no matter the individual circumstances you chance to meet, opportunity in life will undoubtedly always be there for you in some form or another; a byproduct of the vast scope of all possibility in which we all exist. You do not have to somehow think it into existence or attempt to create it out of thin air.

Yet the field of opportunity that is always available to you does reflect your endless potential for creativity. Most certainly,

The act of translating a possibility into an opportunity is an expression of your own creative force in life.

Therefore, gaining access to your innate level of creativity is as simple as opening up to and acting upon the reality of ever present opportunity in your life. Just imagine the self empowering and success enhancing nature of such an "opportunitive" way of thinking and behaving.

---

*"Opportunity motivates people,
and motivated people see opportunity."*

16.

Opportunitivism

Although perhaps seemingly similar words, it is perhaps instructive to point out the distinct differences between the mindset of, what I call, an "opportunitivist" and those of an opportunist or an optimist.

Opportunism

An opportunist, for example, is someone who is willing to take the most advantageous course of action in life irrespective of ethical behavior. Such a practice is fueled by the idea that opportunity is a limited commodity and, when identified, is therefore something to be seized, even at the cost of other people losing out. The life of an opportunist can have a downside however...

When approached in that way—with the objective of "getting yours" before someone else does—the overall influence of ever present opportunity in your life can be deleveraged. This is because, even though significant individual gains might be realized at times through an opportunistic approach, the mindset of opportunism is easily aligned with a scarcity mentality. As a result, your general openness toward and, thus, access to the natural abundance of opportunity in life can be severely restricted. In that way, you thus could rightly say that the limited, "get mine first" modus operandi of some opportunists can in fact attract the negative experience of scarcity into their lives.

Optimism

In comparison, an optimist is someone who believes that goodness pervades reality. In that way, optimism is a form of faith. And having an optimistic faith is a very good thing in life. It allows you to let go of your worries and in turn, while expecting that things will work out for the best, enables you to get on with whatever it is you are doing. And in that sense—positive expectation—optimism also is a form of attraction, in that it invites "good" to happen.

However, although most definitely a positive way of looking at things, the mindset of optimism is, in general, more of a belief about life than an approach toward it. As such, while believing that good things will happen but not necessarily seeking them out, optimists can tend to be more passive than active. In that way optimism—again, being a belief that good is pervasive and that it will occur—is not necessarily a direct catalyst for immediate success. Consequently, although it can (and so often does) play a valuable role within the overall experience of success, optimism is not the key to accelerating the process in which success occurs.

Opportunitivism

In contrast to an opportunist or an optimist, an opportunitivist understands—some, intellectually; although most, intuitively—that the world is set up in a way in which an opportunity can be found at any instant in any situation. And with that realization an opportunitivist further understands the indelible fact that, even though opportunity often initially presents itself in ways that are not immediately apparent, there is always enough opportunity to go around for the people who opt to acknowledge it. This underscores what is one of the principal themes of this book:

> *"You cross the great divide from a scarcity mindset to an abundance mindset in life when you no longer assume that opportunity isn't there but, instead, assume that it is."*

At first glance however, the understanding and approach in life that opportunity is always available—the very essence of opportunitivism—does not make sense to some people. They cite in example routine circumstances or negative events or even dangerous scenarios and then point out that there really is not much, if any, opportunity to be found there. But that is the misinterpretation of a limited awareness. Again, due to the natural progression of energy in life, opportunity is always present whether or not you have the presence of mind to see it.

Such an outlook of abundance is just the opposite of the scarcity mindset of the typical opportunist. And whereas an optimist believes that goodness pervades reality, an opportunitivist looks to take action based on the reality that opportunity is always available. Through such an enlightened and empowering mental approach toward the phenomenon of ever present opportunity in life, an opportunitivist actively stimulates and, thus, accelerates the actual, structural process of success within his or her immediate experience of living.

And just as opportunism and optimism are each a way of looking at life—the former, a mindset of scarce opportunity; the latter, a general belief in goodness— opportunitivism is also an outlook toward living, but one that in essence celebrates the abundance of opportunity. And what a great way to look at life: as a celebration of abundance. And exercising an ability to discover the ever-present but unrealized opportunity that can be found in any situation is an active celebration of great living. Along that compelling line of thought there is an ancient and instructive proverb that says,

"It is man that makes truth great,
not truth that makes man great."

This is to say, the fact that opportunity is abundant is not what counts. What counts is you. That you, as an individual, not only open your mind to the reality that opportunity is always there, but that you take action based on the fact. A true opportunitivist, therefore, is someone who is consistently both open minded and proactive in his or her approach toward the phenomenon of naturally abundant opportunity within his or her todaily process of living.

*"Life offers little guarantee,
but big opportunity."*

17.

A New Definition of Success

One of the recurring themes of this book is that there is more than one definition of success; that because we are different people, there are going to be many different but workable versions of what the concept can mean. However, a central point of the book is that, although it is up to each one of us as an individual to develop our own individual formula for success, because of our common makeup as human beings there are certain truths about how success works that apply to all people. And remember, success is not something you are given; it must in some way be achieved. That is why the three great laws of success have been brought up for detailed discussion within these pages; because together they comprise the basis for what a highly functional process of achievement looks like.

And even though I applaud dozens of individual descriptions of success throughout this work, my longtime consideration of the subject has led me to identify one specific yet generic example of what success most fundamentally means... Looking at it from the vantage of how opportunity actually comes into being—recall the process of natural progression and the individual's role in interpreting the possibilities it presents—the law of acceleration offers you the following new and intriguing definition of success that is applicable to all people:

Success is the
experience of benefit.

An illustration of this is when you say that a particular situation *"worked out"* for you. What you mean is that you experienced some form of benefit in relation to that specific possibility. After all and when you think about the nature of it, an opportunity is simply a possibility that is of benefit to you in some way. This therefore means that...

Opportunity is the
unit of success.

In other words, so goes your experience with opportunity (benefit for you), so goes your experience with success. Consequently, based both on the generally applicable-to-all definition of success as the experience of benefit and on the reality that life is todaily (only happens in the now), the level of your success in life is largely a function of your approach toward the phenomenon of opportunity in your day-to-day process of living. And that is what the law of acceleration is all about.

However, two essential things likely must take place if you are to "accelerate" the experience of success you have within your process of living. First, you must buy into the fundamental nature of opportunity, not as a scarcity event but as an abundance phenomenon; an all pervasive field of ever present and interconnected energy in which you live and operate at all times. Second and as pointed out when discussing the law of action, your commitment must not just be stated, it must also be demonstrated; meaning action is required. Together, these two realities point to the fact that…

Success acceleration is a way of thinking and behaving, both.

Again, when you base your approach to success upon the natural fact that opportunity is always available, you adopt an exceptional and highly functional way of looking at life; not just because of the good it portends, but also because it accurately portrays the way in which the world is set up. Unfortunately, too few people's view of life fits that description. Instead, they are stuck in the rut of not believing that there is enough opportunity to go around. Yet when you see it for what it really is,

A rut is simply that space between latent opportunity and seizing it.

Therefore, if you do in fact look at it that way, any rut in which you find yourself represents a clear opportunity for you to bridge the gap between your unwarranted self-limitations and your personal path of progression by taking appropriately effective action; a scenario that, itself, demonstrates the ever-present nature of opportunity in life.

Still, people unwittingly undermine their actions from the standpoint of opportunity by thinking they do not have that much access to it. They tend to believe that, to get ahead, they must grab for their piece of a limited pie. They do not seem to realize that, rather than grabbing for a limited piece, they only need learn how to "bake more pie"; which, of course, is a metaphor for opening up to what is already there. Yet even when they do begin to understand that opportunity is always available, people often suspect that taking advantage of that actuality must be difficult to do. With that concern in mind, this insightful thought aptly applies:

Simple is physical,
easy is mental.

The reality of naturally abundant opportunity is a simple and uncomplicated fact of nature. Whether or not you have much access to it, however, depends on the six inches between your own two ears. As noted earlier, it all boils down to how you look at it; which is to say, the manner in which you see things. Just as how with action you are the achiever and with attraction you are the receiver, with acceleration—being essentially about your mental approach toward opportunity—it is accurate to say that...

You are the perceiver.

Access to opportunity, therefore, is not about effort but rather about openness. And when looking at how open you are toward the phenomenon of opportunity within your todaily process of living, observing the third law of success will shift you from a position of less access to a position of more access – a great spot from which to formulate your own outstanding yet individual definition of success.

"Mindset dictates behavior.
Behavior dictates process.
And process dictates results.

Thus, mindset dictates results."

18.

Upgrade Your Mindset for Success

Although many people understand and, generally, behave in accordance with the laws of action and attraction in their lives, few also effectively approach life from the standpoint of abundant opportunity. In actual practice, because they are neither familiar with the law of acceleration nor aware of the process of natural progression, they unwittingly operate within a mental paradigm of scarcity. As a result—even though they may believe that the universe itself is abundant—in not embracing the reality that opportunity, although often unseen, is always present, people miss far too much of the inherent benefit, or success, that they might otherwise realize in their lives.

Yet, in spite of those limitations, people do instinctively sense the pitfalls of negativity – powerful emotional inhibitors like worry, doubt, and fear. And they often intuitively grasp the need for adopting an upbeat mental approach for success, whether a "can do" attitude toward their endeavors or an optimistic belief that everything happens for a reason. However the basic reality is that life can sometimes be unreasonable or arbitrary or, at times, seem downright unfair; circumstances which cause you to realize that not everything can be reasoned out positively. That is why it is up to you to bring an opportunitive approach toward the things that take place in your life. With that in mind, here is perhaps my favorite saying, again from John Wooden, about the nature of life relative to the actual experience of living it:

> *"The best things happen to the people who make the best of the things that happen."*

And when tuning in to their mindset for success, you often do hear people make positive-minded statements like *"anything is possible"* and *"attitude is everything"* and other sweepingly optimistic declarations. Literally speaking though, "anything" is not possible (although possibility is infinite); and attitude is not "everything" (although attitude does affect everything). But no matter how you explain them, the positive train of thought behind any such examples generally does have a powerfully good psychological impact on people. In that light, remember the fundamental, often applicable tenet of the second great law of success, the law of attraction:

> *Like energy attracts.*

At a minimum, being positive matters in that way. And certainly, a positive mental practice toward living can eventually translate into tangible results from the standpoint of action in people's lives by coaxing them to adopt some of the following standards notable of highly successful individuals:

Think big. Go for it. Don't quit.

But the basic idea of positive thinking—holding the thought in your mind that things will work out—is not to be confused with the concept of an opportunitive mindset, which is both an understanding *and* an awareness that opportunity is always present. True, the philosophy of positive thinking is a vital source of motivation and encouragement for most people and is therefore an essential component within their success experience. However, on its own, positive thinking does not accelerate the actual process of success; rather, through the self-reinforcing contention that everything will be fine, it simply nurtures the potential of it.

Acceleration, in contrast, occurs when you consciously look at life through the eyes of an opportunitivist – that is, from the viewpoint of defined benefit. To do so, remember that the general definition for success applicable to all people is the experience of benefit. And recall that an opportunity is simply a possibility born out of change that is of benefit to you in some way. And keep in mind that opportunity—any opportunity—can only ever be found or experienced in the present moment...

When you interpret the various circumstances of your life in those ways—essentially, by determining the benefit in whatever change is happening in the moment—you actively stimulate and immediately accelerate your experience of success in real time, not sometime later. In that light, a general comparison of the differences between positive and opportunitive thinking in your approach toward living can be distilled down to this:

Positive thinking
mentally keeps you in the game.

Opportunitive thinking
mentally changes the game.

What this means is that while a positive approach keeps you focused on and striving for eventual success, an opportunitive approach—by increasing both your awareness of and access to latent opportunity—causes you to experience more success, more often. Thus, the comparative advantage of opportunitive thinking over positive thinking is that, in reducing the timeframe necessary to realize a benefit, an opportunitive approach speeds up, or accelerates, your basic cycle of success.

And here is the kicker... Although it is possible to have a positive frame of mind without being opportunitive, it is not possible to possess an opportunitive way of thinking without being positive, too. Fortunately, having an opportunity orientation is not an either/or choice between a positive and an opportunitive mindset; it is an upgrade from the former to the latter that fosters both the constructive attitude of a positive outlook and the productive mode of an opportunitive perspective. So take the opportunity to elevate your game by upgrading your mindset for success. Again, when it comes to giving your best, more than being positive toward life,

Be opportunitive!

Embrace the reality that opportunity is all around you by opening up to and looking for opportunity in any situation. Once you harness such a practice of access to the reality of universal abundance, you will personally realize that there is always opportunity for you in life. Consider the enabling and enriching and, undoubtedly, accelerating effect that such a mindset will have on your day to day experience of success…

V.

The Achievement Dynamic

"An opportunitive mind stimulates intention and energizes action to heighten achievement."

19.

Success in Summation

Throughout history many definitions for success have been asserted and practiced by different people from around the world. However, because of our innate human individuality there is no one correct and absolute definition for success that is the same for everyone. Therefore, for the best of success in life, each individual must develop his or her own individual formula but, in being human, must base that formula on certain definite and specific criteria that are true for all people. Consequently, in relation to your own experience of success there are a few essential laws and principles that are in your best interest to understand and apply.

Although my in-depth look into what constitutes the nature of success in life has been a personal passion spanning many years, my objective has been to refine much of the various and pertinent information into a format that is both concise and useable. This is why I have ultimately focused on what I deem to be the three great laws of success. What makes them great is that, on the one hand, all three laws are fundamental to the experience of success. In that capacity, each can stand alone in greatly and constructively affecting your process of achievement in life. But on the other hand what also makes them great is that these three particular laws work exceedingly well in concert. Together, and as reviewed below, the laws of action, attraction, and acceleration provide a highly practical yet undeniably solid foundation upon which to build your best overall expression of success.

The Law of Action

The law of action is based upon the principle of *cause-and-effect*, which states that *for every action there is an equal and opposite reaction*. Pertaining to the actual physics of what occurs, the law of action is about the quality and quantity of effort you put in relative to the specific steps you take. In other words, it is about *what you do*. In heeding this law you must watch for and manage the opposing self-limitations of under effort and over work; as well as be alert to the pitfalls of idle motion and the allure of quick success. And to experience the living destiny of achieving your goals while you enjoy the process, do not fall into the pattern of letting today slip away while attempting to make tomorrow pay. Simply speaking, you must remember that the process of success is "todaily". Each day you must wake up to appreciate and take advantage of the reality that today is the day!

The Law of Attraction

The law of attraction is based upon the principle of *attention-and-experience*, which observes that *clear intention supports a course of action in that direction*. Dealing with the potential of what could happen, the law of attraction works based on the level of clarity you have surrounding *what you want*. Stimulate your process of attraction by avoiding uninformed assumptions and by staying open to what might be possible. Tune in to the actual workings of attraction in life through an awareness that like energy often attracts, and by remembering your dual capacity as both transmitter and receiver of the mental messages you send. Go beyond willpower to tap your whypower, as great passion is what sustains great success. And develop a success centering relationship with the seminal question by prompting yourself to ask (and answer) the query of what it is you truly want most when considering any dilemma or decision you may face in life.

The Law of Acceleration

Comparatively, the law of acceleration is based upon the principle of *transformation-and-possibility*, which asserts that *all change is opportunity manifesting itself in a new direction.* Having to do with the opportunity, or benefit, found in what occurs, this third law of success is about the perception you bring, or *what you see.* At the basis of this the all affecting process of natural progression (depicting what are the fundamental mechanics of abundance) shows you how pure energy equals ever present opportunity in life. In that way viewing the world, more than simply positive, your outlook in fact becomes opportunitive. This sets the stage in your life for the emergence of an entirely new yet personally applicable definition of success – the experience of benefit. And it upgrades your mindset for success in a way that enables you to better recognize and act upon more opportunity more often... Beginning immediately!

Overview

Each of the three great laws is a necessary cornerstone in the foundation from which to best launch your drive toward success in life. Without question, in actively heeding the first two laws—the law of action and the law of attraction—you build crucial momentum and gain critical direction within your ongoing process of achievement that can eventually lead to success. Yet by consciously observing the third law of success— the law of acceleration—you immediately and more comprehensively tap into the inherent benefits of ever present opportunity in many more aspects of your life. And in welcome consequence you simultaneously enhance and advance, or accelerate, both your personal process of achievement and your individual experience of success within the present moment.

"The essence of life is found in change.
The meaning of life is found in defining change.
The opportunity of life is found in embracing change."

20.

The Untold Promise

Unique in the following way, the third law of success—the law of acceleration—points to one vital, yet normally untapped aspect of the success experience: the way in which you perceive and, therefore, act upon the phenomenon of opportunity in life. Again, at the basis of this and essentially representing the core components of abundance in life, the ever occurring process of natural progression shows how energy, in all its varied yet interconnected and interactive states, creates constant change and, resultantly, endless possibilities that, depending on how you look at things, become ever present opportunity for you. Consequently, and although it may at first seem too incredible to be true, the daily reality for each and every one of us is that...

Opportunity is everywhere!

This amazing fact is the untold promise of life. How so? Well, it is untold because, being relatively unknown, it is not much talked about. Honestly, how many people do you currently know who absolutely believe and operate as if opportunity is everywhere in their lives? And it is a promise because of the abundant good that it suggests for people in their lives; ever present opportunity they can actually access and experience in the now term. For sure, the immediate and substantial benefits of tapping into opportunity is the great part about donning the cap of what I term an "opportuneur", that rare type of person who looks for, identifies, and acts upon opportunity in any situation. Such opportuneurship is in fact a veritable lodestone for the experience of success in life.

Most definitely the theme that, at any point in your life, opportunity is everywhere is in fact meant to be one of the overriding messages of this book; a fundamental, experience altering message that will reshape the way you look at life and modify your approach toward living it. Gone will be the days of scarcity in which your resources for success seem all too few. Here to stay will be the experience of success in which an abundance of opportunity is the rule. In that way you will come to fully and sincerely appreciate that...

Opportunity is the
gift of life.

And all you really need do to make such an untold but fresh promise come true in your life is open your mind to the way the world actually works in relation to the ever abundant nature of opportunity that is always available to you. Again, it is both a way of looking at life and an approach toward living; one that will effectively guide you in your everyday pursuit of excellence. And with such an opportunitive mindset for success you will be quite well suited to take advantage of what is perhaps the one common denominator of life....change. Indeed central to the process of natural progression, change is perhaps the best word to describe life itself. This is because without change you do not have life; which is to say that you will always be facing change in your life. You therefore could say that resisting change is in some way resisting the process of living. Thus it logically follows:

To be really good at life,
be really good at change.

And the reality for all of us, whether or not we appreciate it or even acknowledge it to be true, is that change is always happening. Consequently, although you can attempt to ignore it, you cannot actually avoid it; which is why when discussing the phenomenon of change in their lives I counsel people to...

"Adapt or
be adapted."

Meaning, either consciously embrace change in life or, in essence, be left behind. I saw an example of such thinking while attending an IT symposium. What struck me was the saying, "*Adapt or be hacked.*" Of all people, true professionals in the world of digital technology clearly understand that, because the pace of technological change is occurring so rapidly, they must constantly be adapting or they will quickly fall behind in the never-ending race to innovate and, as a result, lose their competitive advantage.

And because change is constant in life, we each in our own ways face essentially that very same challenge; again, embrace change or be left behind. Whether in terms of becoming the person you can in fact become, or in achieving the specific objectives that you are aiming for, or on the basis of having the kind of life you are truly capable of enjoying, dealing effectively with change will be a major factor in your success. Thus, in looking at this all affecting phenomenon in your life, be clear in your mind that...

Change is a wave of energy.

And it is a wave you either can failingly attempt to ignore by avoiding it, or can struggle against in a self-limiting and unsatisfying swirl of ineffectiveness, or a wave you can flow with and, speaking metaphorically, surf for the ride of your lifetime. Either way, it is the same wave, or pattern, of energy. What is different is the way in which you look at it and, thus, deal with it. In other words, instead of having the forces of change ceaselessly harass and torment you throughout the course of your lifetime, more often than not you can turn the effects of those very same waves of energy toward your own beneficial ends. In this way,

You are the deciding factor
in your own success!

*"Security isn't found in avoiding change,
but in embracing opportunity."*

21.

Choose Success Today

Ultimately, it is you who determines whether or not you take advantage of the reality that change is a wave of energy; an always active natural wonder that you can easily and effectively harness for success. Fundamentally speaking, that ability essentially begins with a clear understanding of what the law of acceleration, again, is essentially about:

> *"Constant change equals*
> *ever present opportunity."*

When you upgrade your mindset and, thus, approach toward living in ways that are consciously in tune with the live, ever abundant nature of opportunity in life—opportunity born of constant change creating endless possibilities—you instantly become a potent force for your own immediate success and, accordingly, your ability to achieve rises. Guided by more than a well meant yet vague assertion that, perhaps someday, you can do anything, you perform based on the specific and more powerful understanding that, as of this very day,

You can do amazing!

And with such a mentality driving your process of achievement forward, it is you who can find the silver lining in any cloud; and you who, when one door closes, can open a window in a new direction. As you progress you will regularly come to experience and enjoy the *wow* of "oppiphany", which is the sudden awareness of a new opportunity presenting itself. You truly can be that person. But again, the choice is entirely up to you...

Choose to accelerate your overall experience of success in life by embracing the basic nature of opportunity and committing to identify it more freely each day. Instead of viewing opportunity as a scattered series of rare events, look at it as an ongoing phenomenon of abundance; an amazing reality borne of the natural and constant interplay of universal energy in all its varying states that characterizes the world in which you live. In going forward, no matter the scenario in which you find yourself, always make a point of asking the question-of-opportunity:

Where's the opportunity?

And then, in recalling that opportunity is in fact three-dimensional—it can happen at any time, in any form, in any place—open your mind to what might be possible in any situation… You will discover that there is always opportunity waiting for you in life. And as you personally live into the basic fact that opportunity is an ever abundant and readily accessible resource, you will quicken and, thus, upgrade your near term experience of success. As a result you will come to realize that…

When looking through the lens of opportunity, one good thing leads to another.

Do you believe that opportunity is in fact everywhere? Are you honestly open to the prospect of opportunity in any set of circumstances you meet? Are you willing to translate the many surprises of life from the standpoint of benefit? Do you think of success, at least in part, as the practical ability to turn lemons into lemonade? If yes, you will live your life in accordance with this rather unknown but basic fact of achievement:

Opportunitivism is a self-propelling mindset for success.

What this means is that an opportunity orientation is a mentality that naturally tends to promote the conscious yet spontaneous translation of possibility into opportunity in any aspect of your life; and which therefore affords you more access to the high level of creativity that you naturally possess. And such a potent mindset for success is more than the positive attitude of an optimist; and it is the opposite of the scarcity perspective of an opportunist. It is an opportunitive way of thinking that, based on a personal and clear awareness that opportunity is present in any situation you happen to face, supports both a constructive and productive approach toward anything you do.

As you journey through your experience of living, strive to upgrade your process of achievement in your own individual ways. In so doing you will develop a growing sense that life not only happens to you but that you happen to life. And you will enjoy the self-fulfilling experience of getting more of what you really want and less of what you just seem to get. In those ways you will exemplify a basic but wise piece of advice that is yet another simple and outstanding formula for success in life:

In going forward,
keep growing forward.

And as you venture forth, always keep in mind that your experience of living is ruled by the physical reality of constant change creating endless possibility within the limited time frame of your lifespan. This means that, although the universal and natural order of things gives you time for plenty, there simply is not enough time for everything. Again, when would you do it all? Therefore, effectively governing your process of achievement in life involves wisely choosing the ways in which you employ the immensely valuable time that you are given, which is a gift only you can give yourself.

By observing the third law of success in conjunction with both the law of action and the law of attraction you will experience a new and dynamic level of achievement; one that synergistically connects what you are doing with why you are doing it with the mindset for doing it well. Such a powerful approach toward living will leverage your time in ways that produce much more benefit in your life; and your days will most assuredly compound into a rewarding expression of success unlike anything you have ever experienced before. Just as promised, you will come to appreciate the amazing reality in your life that...

Opportunity is everywhere!

So with a mind toward giving your very best, resolve to be the key ingredient in your own success. Combine an "active" and "attractive" and "opportunitive" approach toward your process of achievement in life and, in welcome result, step out of the shadow of self-limitation into the light of your own greatness.

Choose success today.

Opportunity Lexicon

Opportunity: **op•por•tu•ni•ty** (op′ ər too′ ni tē), noun: 1. an appropriate or favorable time or occasion. 2. a situation or condition favorable for attainment of a goal. 3. a good position, chance, or prospect, as for advancement or success.

Optimism: **op•ti•mism** (op′ tə miz əm), noun: the belief that goodness pervades reality.

Optimistic: **op•ti•mis•tic** (op′ tə mis′ tik), adjective: disposed to take a favorable view of events or conditions and to expect a most favorable outcome.

Optimist: **op•ti•mist** (op′ tə mist), noun: a person who holds the belief or doctrine of optimism and who is optimistic.

Opportunism: **op•por•tun•ism** (op′ ər too′ niz əm), noun: the policy or practice of adapting actions, decisions, etc., to expediency or effectiveness regardless of the sacrifice of ethical principles.

Opportunistic: **op•por•tun•is•tic** (op′ ər too nis′ tik), adjective: willing to take the most advantageous course of action irrespective of ethical behavior.

Opportunist: **op•por•tun•ist** (op′ ər too′ nist), noun: a person who practices the policy of opportunism and who is opportunistic.

Opportunitivism: op•por•tu•ni•tiv•ism (op′ ər too′ ni ti viz əm), noun: the understanding that, universally, opportunity is latent and can thus be found at any instant, in any place, and in any form.

Opportunitive: op•por•tu•ni•tive (op′ ər too′ ni tiv), adjective: the mindset that opportunity is everywhere; inclined to look for opportunity in any situation, circumstance, or event.

Opportunitivist: op•por•tu•ni•tiv•ist (op′ ər too′ ni ti vist), noun: a person who embodies opportuntivism and who is opportunitivistic.

Opportuneur: op•por•tu•neur (op′ ər too nûr′), noun: a person who looks for, identifies, and acts upon opportunity in any scenario, often when others don't.

Opportuneurship: op•por•tu•neur•ship (op′ ər too nûr′ ship), noun: the practice of opening up to the nature of opportunity in life, and the resultant tendency to discover benefit no matter what happens.

Oppiphany: op•piph•a•ny (op pif′ ə nē), noun: a sudden, intuitive perception or insight into the presence and nature of a new opportunity.

<u>**Notes**</u>

22472411R00086

Made in the USA
San Bernardino, CA
08 July 2015